TRAINING YOUR MIND TO FOCUS ON THE SOLUTION

APPLIED FREEDOM TECHNOLOGIES

THE HIS-STORY

MICHAEL WYATT AKA "FREEDOM"

A F Technologies Inc.

The opinions expressed in this manuscript are solely the opinions of the author and do not represent the opinions or thoughts of the publisher. The author has represented and warranted full ownership and/or legal right to publish all the materials in this book.

Applied Freedom Technologies The His-Story
Training Your Mind to Focus on the Solution

v2.0

A F Technologies Inc.

ISBN: 978-0-578-13553-3

PRINTED IN THE UNITED STATES OF AMERICA

Contents

Preface by Freedom

I wrote this book to provide an overview of the foundation for Applied Freedom Technologies (AFT), including my history as its founder. AFT is a tri-part orchestration of tools, techniques, strategies, and insight which when accepted and applied will allow any individual to manifest the lifestyle they want to have. There are three primary areas addressed in AFT: 1) Body and Mind, 2) Spirit or Source, and 3) Operating in Commerce. (www.myaft.net)

The majority of what resulted in the creation of AFT took place over a six year period in my life, however some of the events and the results of those events were influenced by my early years. From a very young age, I felt that something was missing in this life experience; there seemed to be pieces of the puzzle that did not fit properly or were omitted. I had so many questions about unexplained occurrences and believed that the answers existed somewhere.

I bought the story that if you learn right from wrong, do what is right, go to school, get an education (hopefully a good one), work hard, and be fair, things in this life will work out well for you. I believe this is still generally what is taught today.

One of the primary reasons we want to do what is good and right is because of what religion teaches us about the will of God, and what God wants us to be. I was taught about God, I was taught about the Devil, and that there is a Heaven which I should want to strive toward and Hell - which if I had one smart brain cell or just did not want to burn, I should want to stay away from. Religious instruction left a lot of gaps for me growing up, but when I was young I wanted to please those around me (parents, etc.). When you / I live in a society with norms and traditions, we accept dominate thought as correct and expect to be happy. AFT ultimately came about because I was trying to follow the way of God as I had been taught.

You will undoubtedly come to the conclusion at some point while reading this book that my beliefs have changed. The reason for the change is pressure. Just as it takes an extreme amount of pressure to change a piece of coal into a diamond it took an extreme amount of pressure for me to view life from a different perspective. I came to a realization that many societal traditions, laws, rules, statutes, beliefs, and norms simply are not the truth and would not provide the expected results, which are simply put: a happy life.

If you have ever felt like something was out of place or just does not seem to get better in your life, or if you feel like your life is being controlled by society or your environment, you will be glad to receive the information contained in the pages that follow. I learned the hard way but it does not have to be the same for you.

As you read through this book it is my intention that you receive the empowerment to be in control of your life. You are the center of your life and have the ability by your deliberate thought to create the situations in your life experience that you desire.

AFT is a system in which I have coordinated many of the processes I used to gain direct influence on what happens in my life. I tell the story of the foundation of AFT because I want you to understand that challenges can and will come in your life but you always have a choice. There were key points during a six year stretch in my life where my perspective changed and I give you the sources that influenced, in part, those changes. This is done intentionally so you can go directly to the sources I used to start a positive change for yourself now.

The Applied Freedom Technologies system is uniquely designed to direct you toward the path for the lifestyle you want for yourself. I am truly excited for those who have been attracted to the information in the following chapters and hope you will take what is available for you to live this awesome physical life experience on your own terms from this point forward.

Thank you for reading; live an awesome life.

CHAPTER 1

Background - This Was Not the Beginning

How does someone rack up over $260,000 in credit card debt? It is not as outlandish as you may think; I know from personal experience. Of course I never set out to accumulate this kind of debt, however, once I did, I needed to intentionally change my way of thinking to get out of it. You will probably have to change the way you think in order to change a situation in your life. The good news is there are more tools available today than ever before to assist you in making the change.

I grew up in a family-owned construction business, and for me that meant working on a consistent basis every summer since I was twelve years old. Even before the age of twelve I worked with my Dad on weekends or when I was on vacation from school. My Dad worked a lot; at least that was the way it seemed to me. I thought it was natural to be working whenever I could. It did not dawn on me until looking back later that I could have been out playing with my friends. The work mentality has been with me all my life, which is not a horrible thing unless there is no fun to balance it off. I think we all become subjects of our environment which also plays a large role in how we think and how much we may need to change our thinking before we can find out who we are meant to be.

I applied for and received my first credit card at age seventeen, an American Express Gold Card. It was my most cherished card because in the 1970's, the Gold Card represented a bit of status, especially for a seventeen year old. My reason for wanting Amex Gold Card status at that age is probably what led to my financial trouble later in life. It might have been a little strange, but growing up at that time I did not want to owe anybody any money. I remember my Dad bought me my first car at age sixteen, when I got my license. I think my brothers and sister expected that and we all got it, so I guess we were all spoiled to some extent. My second car was a 280z. I think it was two years old but it was nice. My Dad paid the down payment, and I made the monthly payments. I did not feel comfortable until I had enough money in the bank to pay that car off in full if I wanted to. I believe my thinking probably made sense, but the extreme application of it would cause a problem when it came time for me to buy a house unless I paid cash, which was not likely.

Since that time I have possessed many credit cards. I became what I call a credit card collector. My credit was excellent so companies just kept sending me offers for more cards. At the height of my card collecting, which was around 2002 or 2003, I must have had between 40 and 50 credit cards (it could have been more). My total available credit on the cards was well over $400,000.00.

I did not have a lot of disposable income at that time but I had lots of credit cards and good credit because I always paid my bills on time. I did not want to owe anyone any money. Of all the credit cards I had there was only one card that I paid an annual fee to keep and that was my American Express Gold Card. I even had four or five other American Express credit cards, all with no annual fee. If any of the card issuing companies wanted to charge me a fee I would just cancel the card. I did not realize that even though I had always been very good at managing my finances I was really playing with fire and as anyone who has played with fire knows, sooner or later you will get burned.

Our thoughts do create our reality and even though I did not know what my thoughts were creating for me at that time it does not mean I was not responsible for the outcome.

CHAPTER 2

A Long Walk with God

I was always trying to get ahead to move up in life and live at a more abundant level. I went to church and paid my tithes. I actually gave ten percent of my income to the church I attended for many years of my life. I was raised in the church so to speak, but let it go until my oldest son was around two years old. My mom was from the south and we grew up with Southern Baptist tinges like, "the only right Christian is a Baptist Christian." We did not believe in that "being filled with the Holy Spirit and speaking with other tongues stuff;" that was spooky.

I had not really thought about this before now but my mom probably should not have been married to my dad. My dad worked hard and he played hard (he liked to party). I know he knew what the outside of a church looked like because we had plastered many of them, but I never saw my dad on the inside of a church until he was retired and in his seventies. Because of my dad I sometimes wondered if maybe I did not need church. However, I had another son on the way and my life still was not where I wanted it to be, so I turned myself and my family back to God and the Bible.

During that period of my life I read the Bible cover to cover more than once. I listened and looked for the interpretation and understanding of the scriptures that made sense and felt right to me. I wanted the benefits of being a child of God, a child of the King who was creator of all things.

My journey to live my life the way the Bible laid it out was not without conflict. There are a lot of don'ts in the Bible and some of those don'ts I liked to do, so I had to battle with myself. You could call it a battle between my conscious mind and my subconscious mind. That was an interesting battle as I guess it is for most people who have to deal with it. I found out later why this battle is so hard. Most of what all people do comes from programs or tracks which are embedded or etched into our minds when we are children. It was a little hard to come to terms with this but it is scientific fact that 95 to 99 percent of adult behavior is due to programs we received (downloaded) in to our subconscious mind during the first six months to six years of our life here on earth.

This could be a good thing or bad thing depending on where the programs you are running have come from and what you are trying to achieve in your life right now. For me there were some things I liked to watch but God vid the Bible via the Pastor was telling me I should not watch any more or even want to watch, if I am a good Christian. Now with consistent effort using the conscious mind we (humans) are able to overwrite the old thoughts and old programs and fortunately today there are many tools available to assist in the process of retraining the subconscious mind. However if you do not know where the conflict in your mind is coming from and many times, even if you do, the old programs still win. The process for overwriting old programs can be complicated.

I studied and searched for two years, maybe a little longer before I decided on a church with a Pastor/Teacher who I believed really knew what he was talking about and had a lifestyle of blessings from God to back it up.

I became filled with the Holy Spirit as a result of my contact with this particular Pastor, which happened before we joined his church. I had always heard bad things about being filled with the Holy Spirit and speaking with other tongues. It was said to be like devil worship or something like that. When I was nine or ten a cousin of mine got filled with the Holy Spirit and it was a dark and spooky event which seemed to fit right in with what I had heard. When it happened we were in a little run down house on a little run down street. I remember the grass in the yard being dry and tall; the house just seemed shabby on the outside and on the inside. We were there during the daytime, but inside the house was still dimly lit. I did not notice anything different with my cousin afterward, except that he could speak words that neither he nor I could understand. I just figured we were all a little strange.

I will say that with correct knowledge and teaching comes better understanding. I allowed this infilling of the Holy Spirit to take place within me (of course this was many years later), and it was one of the most powerful, empowering experiences I have ever had in my life. I was filled with power, strength, and clarity. It was an incredible feeling that lasted about three days, and then it was gone. I have tried for many years to get the feeling back but have never been able to sustain it like that for any length of time at that level.

My family and I stayed with that church for eight years even though it was located about forty minutes from where we lived. We would go every Sunday and often an additional day of the week for Bible study or if there was something else going on at the church. We were introduced to Pastors from other ministries and I felt really good about my spiritual life. I believed I had a good understanding of the Bible and I received my own revelations from reading the scriptures, but my financial life just seemed to stay in the same place. If our finances dipped a little God would always bring it back to our norm. If it looked like we were about to move up to a better standard of living, I guess it was Satan who brought us back down because God would not do that to us. Nevertheless we seemed to stay at the same level.

I may have just ignored the fact that many of the people I knew in the church were still facing the same issues. My issue was primarily financial which was probably the dominant challenge for most; but there were also those experiencing health, relationship issues, or something else. It did not seem that many were living the abundant life of the pastor no matter how long they had been there, and since God is not a respecter of persons then it must have been something else keeping the blessings from me and the majority of the other people attending the church.

I used to wonder if other people gained more benefits by turning to God after their life had been jacked up by drugs or alcohol. I had not done those kinds of things before turning to God to heal and save me. I wondered if I missed out on some fun I should have had. Even though the people I am referring to really needed help to get their lives back on a better track, they all seemed to have some fun stories about the times when they were "bad." I saw myself and my life as pretty much "Mr. Straight Laces."

I learned a lot from the Pastors I became acquainted with and really practiced what I was learning so that God would answer my prayers the same way He appeared to be answering theirs. My prayers didn't always seem to work. When my prayers were not answered, I believed that either I was not doing something right or I was just not worthy yet.

In my mind I knew what I was doing and more importantly what I had done in the past. That is probably what kept my prayers from being answered. In my mind those things would just get regurgitated. I would have flashed back on things I would like to forget, but have not figured out how to bury. The Bible says God has forgiven me, but I have not figured out how to tell my mind to let go. I know now that training your mind to focus on the solution is a way to override the things you want to bury, but I did not learn that until much later in life. The Bible does say "look not at the things that are seen but at the things that are unseen for the things that are seen are temporal and the things that are unseen are eternal" (2 Corinthians 4:18). Maybe that is the Bible version of training your mind to focus on the solution.

CHAPTER **3**

Working in the Financial Industry

Although I had grown up in the family business, construction was never really my cup of tea. My Dad started the business when we were young. I was very proud of him and what he had accomplished and never wanted to let my Dad down, in fact most of what I did was based on his expectation that I would take over what he had started. But when I got to my mid-to-late thirties I decided to let it go and pursue what I always thought I wanted, which was to be in the financial industry working and dealing with money. Apparently I have a tendency to stay with jobs, people, or situations longer than I should or when the benefit for me has diminished. Now I believe it was due to a loyalty factor from old embedded programming. I would have changed this long ago had I known how the mind works and that I had the power to change old programs running in my subconscious mind.

From the time I was very young I always wanted to work in the financial industry. If I had not grown up with a job already waiting for me I would have pursued the idea of working in finance a lot sooner than I did and might have been more successful in that pursuit.

I dreamt of being a stock broker, sitting behind the desk, watching the stock market on my computer, making trades and making money. That is what I wanted. For the most part that is what I got. Let me tell you how the law of attraction got me there.

I left the family business in my late thirties. It was a challenge starting from almost scratch. I had some credits toward my business degree since I had been in and out of college since I left high school many years before. I landed a job with a large Insurance Company - my first real job outside the family business. I did not really think of the insurance business as being in the finance industry but in my time working with this company I learned about mutual funds, annuities, and variable life insurance products.

They were essentially financial instruments with limits and restrictions which meant they had to be classified as insurance products. I learned about these things in school but real world experience is something I appreciated a lot more. One thing that stuck with me is that even today, every family no matter what race, religion, or background, is one generation away from setting up future generations for financial security for life.

That was an exciting and tough time for me, because I had never worked for another company before. It was also difficult to get clients. I thought I was good with people but persuading people to buy something even when it had great benefits for them and their family was tough for me. I was able to segue my start in the insurance business to the area of finance as a financial consultant, which is what I really wanted to do.

During this time I was deep into studying and applying what I learned in church to have an abundant lifestyle. I wanted a good life with enough money to do whatever I wanted, whenever I wanted. The Bible said it was there for me so I just needed to know exactly how to get it.

Working at the Insurance Company was good but it was not the picture that I had for myself. Remember, I wanted to be sitting behind my desk watching the stock charts on my computer, making trades and making money, not searching for ways to get families and businesses to buy insurance. At that time the next big thing coming was going to be assets under management. We received our own personal laptop computers to carry with us on appointments to enhance our stature and productivity. We were on the cutting edge with insurance and would soon need to be series seven licensed so we could offer our clients the complete package with stocks included. This was nice but I wanted it immediately, I just needed to know how to make it happen.

A Pastor that I was introduced to through my home church presented the answer I was looking for. He presented me with the tools and processes to use with visualization, prayer, and how to reprogram the brain with new thought processes that are in line with the Word of God.

I applied the process to my life and it was working: the doors were opening for me to get the position I wanted to be in and I was excited. I was using what I had learned and I believed it to the point of knowing that what I wanted was something that was meant for me to have. I know now it was not I who orchestrated this situation but we create our own reality by our thoughts and the universe orchestrates situations to bring us what we want.

I did not understand the complete process or how it worked at that time but I was able to land a position with a leading Financial Company and they actually paid me to study for and take my series seven exam.

This was really an exciting time for me. I was in the position I had visualized myself being in. I had my desk, my office, and my computer with the best possible software for tracking stocks. It was everything I could have wanted it to be, although a bit overwhelming, and I was happy.

I did not include all the details about how I used the Pastor's series to get to where I wanted to be. But after learning much later how the law of attraction works I recognize the processes or methods of visualization in this series taught by the Pastor were not exclusive to the Bible, in fact it probably existed before the Bible and there are other steps that when included will make the process work better. This process of creating what you want works regardless of your religious inclination; it works even if you have no religion. The mind is designed to function in a certain way and if I use my mind to think in a consistent manner, it would not be my prayers that get answered but my thoughts. Training your mind to focus on the solution is very powerful and is the key to the lifestyle you want to live. (www.myaft.net)

Having made it to the career I wanted to be in was not enough. I was still missing key instructions, including how to maintain my position. I was not able to do that because I did not know what to do next. At the time I thought it was because I did not know enough people who had enough money for me to meet the quotas needed to make management happy. But I know now that was not the reason. Had I known then what I know now, it would have been easier for me to meet whatever standards were required. I probably would have had an awesome rest-of-my-life experience, but then I might have also missed the knowledge that I have come to know now. Universal law is of far greater value than almost anything you could ever want to know, it should be the foundation upon which you build. It is by the understanding of universal law that one creates their reality on this planet.

CHAPTER 4

The Same Old Struggles

I met a lot of good and caring people at my church. One very influential and beneficial person to me was the men's fellowship president. He seemed to help everyone he came in contact with, and it meant a lot that he was caring and loving in a Godly way toward me. I grew up with three brothers and I considered him my fourth. It was nice being around him and during difficult times; he would listen and give me ideas.

One of the many qualities he had was that he was a great speaker, and was really engaging and fun. He told me this skill or knack was brought to light during his time working for a large delivery company.

When he talked about this company, his stories really stuck with me. I remembered always seeing their trucks moving about and would pass by their building a lot during the time I worked in the family business. At this particular time in early 2000 I was having a tough time in the financial department again, at least according to my perception that I must have enough money in the bank to pay off my car in full (even if there were four years of payments left). For me it was not only an issue of paying monthly bills; I was looking toward the future.

I had left the family business, I had left the large insurance company, I had pretty much been given my walking papers at the large financial firm, and I had tried working with a couple other financial companies which just did not work out for me.

I had also been doing some consulting and estimating for a few construction companies but income was neither regular nor consistent. I remember during those times I would sit and think about how my life might have been easier if I had not grown up in a family business but had gone to work for a large company like the delivery company my friend worked for. I would have had a 401k plan, decent hours, been a manager or supervisor with benefits and would have probably become an instant millionaire when the stock went public in the late 90's. I thought I could have been living a comfortable life with my family because the grass always looks greener on the other side. That was not actually the case. At this point I did not even have medical insurance for my children, not to mention my wife or myself. It is easy for me to look back and see that my thoughts were not in the right place at that time. If I had known the power in directing my thoughts, I would have decided on a different course.

I remember having to take my sons to a clinic using California Healthy Families, which was a state sponsored program that assisted low-income families in getting decent medical care. I am not knocking Healthy Families but I felt like a failure having to do that. I had a family member at that time who was working for a large delivery company and he told me they were hiring. The positions available were part-time but that was still a good option because part-timers at this company receive medical benefits and I wanted real medical coverage for my family. I also figured if I was only working part-time at night. I could go to school during the day and finish up my bachelor's degree, which I had been working on and off since I finished High School.

I went in, filled out the application, went for the interview, and never received a call. I had included my relative on some portion of the paperwork and found out later that was probably the reason I never got a call back.

I tried again about four months later and did not include any reference, and received a call pretty quickly. My first day working for that company was October 31, 2000.

CHAPTER 5

Introspective: *You Mean It Is Not About Me?*

I always believed that because I was raised up in a family business, that I missed out on some of the growth curve that many kids go through, from getting their first paper route or baby-sitting job to working at a fast food joint, department store, or movie theater and transitioning into something more challenging and demanding as they grow up.

I do appreciate the fact that I did not have to go and find a job, especially because I was making good money working for my Dad during my early teens. However, I still believe the social interaction of working around kids my age and the process of applying, interviewing, competing and being recognized or scolded may have served me in some fashion. I have for the most part been considered a quiet kind of fellow although I do not believe that I am shy. I believe the increased social interaction would have made a difference in my demeanor.

I grew up working with a lot of older men who instructed, trained, and told me what to do, so when the point of transition came for me to have authority, I think it was a little more difficult for me to supervise and manage my father's older workers. My Dad was not what I would call a traditional teacher. I know a lot of the things he did, but I could not tell you why he did them. Some of the things made sense to me and some did not. He did not have much structure in his methods, but it worked for him.

I have always had a sense of fairness, because I thought being fair and treating people fairly is the right way to be. One of the difficulties for me was to accept the fact that even when I know I was being fair I could not assume that whomever I was working with would accept my being fair as fair. We had employees who had their own agenda and for them being fair meant them winning and me losing. It could be something as simple as how long a 15 minute break is. They would think the break started when they took the first bite of a sandwich and ended 5 to 10 minutes after they should have been back at work, not to mention going to the bathroom once the break is over

CHAPTER 6

The Job Growth Curve

I had to go through something similar to that growth curve when I was a little older and carried a lot more responsibility.

I once worked as a delivery guy using my own truck. Most of it was courier work, delivering small items like documents and blueprints. It was not necessarily hard work but it did make me both appreciate and resent growing up in the family business.

I appreciated it because I did not have to do this kind of entry level work but I resented my time with the family business because I found myself doing entry level work much later in life.

On one particular day I recall I was delivering cookies. These were not just any cookies but the big birthday cookies that are the size of a dinner plate - actually a little larger than that. I do not recall exactly how much money I was going to make from deliveries that day but I did know that by around twelve noon I was working for nothing. The three cookie deliveries seemed to be in three different parts of the world. I was using my map book as there were no GPS systems at that time. I have always been good with directions and finding locations because I spent many hours on the road going from job to job working in the family business. I easily put a thousand miles a week on my truck.

On this day the information on the map and what I was seeing did not seem to match up; the area must have been relatively new. I noticed several toll booths to get on and off the highways which I made an effort to avoid. I had the cookies in the cab with me but I could not keep the balloons up front with me because they were helium filled and as they bounced around in the cab they obstructed my view. I let them fly out the window - some on the passenger side, some through the little window behind me.

The problem was the more I drove, the more the wind made the balloons bounce around outside my windows. They were making a lot of noise and I was afraid I was going to lose some of them. In my haste to get the job completed and without clear directions I ended up taking one of the toll roads.

The first toll booth did not appear to be manned; in fact it did not even look like it was operational. As I got closer to a point where I could not turn back if I wanted to, I could see that it was not manned but it did have a funnel where you were supposed to toss in your coins. The toll was about $.50 or $.60 cents and I did not have any change. Like I said, it was not manned so I'm thinking what choice do I have, I will have to go through. I went through without putting money in and I do not believe I got three feet beyond the toll booth before red lights started flashing, sirens were sounding and pictures were being taken of me in my truck. I was pretty sure that meant I was going to get a ticket down the line somewhere. I was already not going to make any money that day but now I would have to pay out money on top of that. I was ready to call it quits for the day, but since I had come that far, I at least had to make the final cookie delivery. I went on with that final delivery to make, the balloons still bouncing around in the back and having to go back through the toll road.

Heading back the opposite direction, the road had a section where the driver could go through the booth to pay like the one I already had my picture taken in or you could just stay on the highway if you had a speed pass module in your car. I did not have a speed pass module in my truck, but I did not have change for the toll booth either, so I figured I would just get my picture taken this time without the flashing lights and sirens and shoot myself when I got home (just kidding on the shoot myself part).

I sped through on the way to the last cookie delivery, but before I got off the highway I lost the balloons for my cookie. They just went flying away in the air probably back to the toll booth. Needless to say, I had enough for that day. I did deliver the cookie and the lady did not mention anything about not having any balloons so I did not say anything either. I called the city regarding the amount of the tickets for the toll roads and was told they were $180.00. The good note is I waited for weeks and never received a ticket.

One of the other odd jobs I took was the installation of satellite dishes. For me this job was a pain in the butt; it was very difficult to get and keep a signal locked in. I worked at this job for a couple of weeks without getting paid because the guy I was working for did not have the money. I stopped working and continued to call the guy to get the money he owed me.

One thing my Dad never did was keep any employee waiting on their money; he always paid them on time, so I was really pissed at this guy. When he finally said he had my money we met at a gas station. I will always remember this. Things were really tight for me and I wanted the money I had earned. When I met with him and he was trying to short me on the money I had worked for, I was like a bull seeing red. He said he had to go back or have someone go back and fix a job I had completed. I was not buying that because he should have called me to go back out and repair it.

I am not a violent person but I punched this guy right in the chin. We were going to fight right there at the gas station, but somehow I just got back in my truck and left. He was pretty angry, but I was angry too and scared because that was out of character for me and I did not know what to expect. My wife and I actually went to the police station in that city to try and preempt anything that might happen, but apparently he never reported it.

It was like my life was a cartoon at this point. I was Wiley Coyote and no matter what I came up with or tried to do the anvil just kept falling back on my head. It was like bad things attracting more bad things. I see now that was actually universal law in effect, situations attracting more like situations.

What I did not know was the power to change that was within me the entire time.

The point I want to make here is that in doing this job and the other odd jobs I was trying to make things happen for myself. I had a family to support so I had to do whatever hustle I could manage to make money. It was all about taking action. Had I known there was a better, easier way and it was with me at every moment I would have taken it. But no one ever told me I could think my way to a better situation. No one told me, that just by changing my thoughts from stress, struggle and lack to prosperity, joy and plenty, I could have changed my situation.

I was pretty fed up with the odd job thing and wanted and needed something to bring a consistent income in a hurry. This was around the time of my second application to the delivery company.

CHAPTER 7

Supernatural Events or *Just Strange Things That Happen to Me*

Several things have happened to me over the years which firmly convinced me that there is more to this physical life experience than anyone has ever come close to explaining to me. I became aware at some point that if I could get myself to believe something and take action based on those beliefs, I would be more comfortable taking those actions. This is how you overwrite old programming. For example, at one point in my life I wanted to speak Spanish well and be comfortable doing that. I was not what most people would call proficient, but I did take Spanish in high school and I had also purchased a teaching tape series to help me learn to speak Spanish. I knew enough to speak it but I did not feel right doing it. So one day I made a decision I was going to speak it and be confident doing it. I believed the best way to really get it was to speak it during my daily activities.

As much as I had opportunity I would speak Spanish. I went in to stores, especially places to get fast food and if I thought the workers spoke Spanish I would speak Spanish. I was not comfortable at first but I was determined to make it natural.

It was interesting. I would get funny looks and I could tell the workers were a little shocked but after a little while it was fun. Even though my Spanish was not always right, I knew that the people I spoke with appreciated me speaking their language and they gave me pointers to get better. I only pursued this idea on a limited scale, because I really did not understand the power of what I believed to be true.

When I was in junior high school, a life-event that has stayed with me since it happened clearly demonstrated that there are other sources of power we have access to, but often do not use, because we have not learned how. The truth is there are sources of power available for us to benefit from, the issue preventing us from accessing them is control. If your mind is free and you know it you cannot be controlled. That does not mean you or anyone else will be out of control or at the mercy of someone more powerful than you. There is someone in control of your society no matter where you live, and their fear is that if you choose not to be controlled, you will discover they can no longer control you. That should give you a feeling of liberation but society has brainwashed many into fear, lack of protection, lack of food, and lack of peace. Life should be fun; if it is not, it is because you are not thinking correctly. When you learn to think correctly your life will be fun; universal law demands it.

I was in the eighth grade, and it was a typical morning on the upper field area of the school I attended. The kids would gather, some talked and some played basketball or a variety of other games before the bell rang to go to homeroom. I went over to the bleachers where a bunch of guys were doing this weird lifting thing. They appeared to lift a guy like he was light as a feather using only their index fingers. One guy sat on the bottom bench and two guys had their index fingers under the sitting guy's armpits and another two guys had their index fingers placed at the bend of the sitting guy's knees.

Now just watching what they were doing, I knew it had to be a trick and I wanted to know what it was. I chose to be next to see how this would work on me. I sat down on the bottom bleacher, my legs about shoulder width apart and my arms straight out in front of me at shoulder level. Before they put their fingers in position to lift me up they did this thing over my head, I could not see what they were doing, but I knew what they were doing because I watched them do the same thing to other guys before me. What they did was each guy would put a hand over my head palm down fingers together (like you would if you were giving a high five). There was about 3 to 5 or 4 to 6 inches of space between each hand and they could not touch; whatever order was used to start was repeated until all eight hands were over my head. I had a weird feeling at the top of my head, I felt clear and light. They removed their hands in the reverse order that they were put up and then each guy positioned his index fingers together with the other fingers locked together at one of the four spots: right side armpit, right side under the knee, left side armpit, left side under the knee and they proceeded to lift me up about four feet in the air. I felt as light as a feather. That event to this day is still an incredible experience but that was not all.

I decided to participate as one of the guys doing the lifting and this was even more amazing because the guy we lifted weighed was well over three hundred and fifty pounds. I do not believe any of us weighed over one hundred and twenty pounds and even if we did, we lifted this three hundred and fifty pound guy with our index fingers!

Another situation where I used the power of my mind to create was when I played baseball in little league. I was pretty good; I had even gone to the little league world series at age eleven with our little league all-star team.

When I was twelve I hit two homeruns in one game twice, and I had one homerun against this particular team. We had another game coming up against this team and before that game was played I knew without a doubt, because I had already established in my mind, that this team owed me a homerun. I knew that I would hit a homerun at some point during that game. The interesting and unmistakable reality for me here was: "that team owes me a homerun." It was so firm in my mind that I created it and I hit another homerun against them.

I had come to recognize that my thoughts throughout my life were in fact the pre-cursers to what had taken place in my life. This came to light for me as I studied and learned my Pastor's teaching along with scriptures and examples throughout the Bible.

It was easy to see when looking back at my life. My issue or challenge was how to get what I wanted moving forward.

CHAPTER **8**

Bad Thoughts About Carrying Money

The next example of the law of attraction in my life is a situation I would have avoided at all costs. I have included it here just to demonstrate the working of the law of attraction in the lives of people by default and how that can result in life threatening situations and even death.

One of the issues I had with money I relate to My Dad. I did not understand it for a very long time, easily most of my adult life, but it was like the law of gravity or the law of attraction. It really does not matter whether or not you understand the law or intentionally apply it or not, the laws will act on you by default (and in my case it was not for my benefit).

As I mentioned previously my Dad was a businessman. Whether that was the reason he always carried around a big wad of money or not, I do not know, I never asked him. He always kept hundred dollar bills folded or rolled to the outside so whenever he took the wad out of his pocket you could see the hundreds. I am not talking about one or two hundred-dollar bills, there were typically ten, fifteen or twenty of those before you got to the fifties or twenties.

I would usually only carry a small amount of cash with me. If I had three twenties, a ten, and a five I thought I was good. I always had my credit cards with my large limits so I felt I always had access to money if I needed it. During the days when I was running a larger part of the everyday activities of the business I would carry around a cashier's check or checks in my wallet for one thousand to five thousand dollars' worth but I was not comfortable carrying around a lot of cash.

I realized that my discomfort with carrying cash was the reason in large part why I could not seem to gain a foot hold on accumulating cash (money). Money always seemed to be a struggle for me. I rarely had that much cash with me. Once I realized this I understood why money never seemed to be an issue for my Dad; he was always comfortable with cash, and he always had money.

He made no effort to hide the fact that he had a wad of money in his pocket. When he went to pay for something he just took that wad of money out. He took the rubber band off, and flipped open the wad, revealing the one hundred dollar bills that were always on the outside. Whenever he pulled it out, whoever was around would easily see he carried bank.

To my knowledge, my Dad never had any fear or worries about carrying his money around like that. Everybody knew he did that and my Dad was a very charismatic and popular guy. To the best of my knowledge, he never got robbed or attacked because he carried his money in that manner.

I did not like him doing that. I was afraid someone would try to attack him for his money at some point. I walked around uncomfortable with that prospect in my mind for many years. We also dealt with a lot of cash in our business and many times I felt vulnerable because in my mind that was dangerous. I really did not think about what that feeling had produced in me until many years later when I had been studying the law of attraction for about a year or more.

I cannot tell you where the discomfort came from, it could have come from watching too much television or something. I know it did not come from my Dad. Looking back I wish I would have asked him why he did that, and why he did not appear to be concerned about any danger stemming from it. If I had these answers I probably could have stopped the law of attraction before it brought my fears and concerns into manifestation.

By now you have probably anticipated what happened. One Friday, a payday for us, I put the payroll together as was the normal situation. Most of the time we would pay the guys at a job site or they would come by the house after work. Paying the guys on the job was fine, but having them come by the house over time (a long time) became a problem. Some guys like to have a drink after work and that contributed to the problem. It was the norm for us to have five, six, or more crews working in different job locations so it was not possible for me to get to all of them in enough time.

I believe we were meeting at a park near the house to pay the men, so I would have to put the payroll together and leave the protection of the house. This particular day my thoughts, which I take responsibility for now, created what I was concerned about. I was about to get in my truck with the briefcase. As I opened my door, a van came racing up to me and the side door opened. I saw a guy kneeling down with a gun. As I tried to turn away, he fired. They took my briefcase and all that was in it.

I had been shot almost point blank. The bullet went completely through me and it came out on the right side of my chest. If I had not turned, you would not be reading this right now. I was in intensive care for three days, and then I walked out of the hospital. It was not my time to die.

The point is that I have given you another life-altering situation I experienced where the universal laws, specifically the law of attraction, had a major influence on what happened in my life. I can look back and say with confidence I created these situations by my thought processes at that time.

There are many more events that took place prior to and since the above situation but during the events of my "six year stretch" I learned that I am in control of what happens to me. I can look at what happened and know why it happened.

If you think about situations in your life you will come to the same conclusion, that your thoughts create your reality.

CHAPTER **9**

Six Year Stretch: *"The Critical Time"*

I am at a place of ultimate peace today because of a six year stretch in my life. As a result of this six year period I came to an understanding of why I am here and how to create the life style I want for me while I am here in this physical world. I also expect to be living the lifestyle I want in the future because of what I have learned and experienced during that stretch of time.

In January 2006 I expected to leave whatever issues or struggles I had with finances in the past. In 2005 we refinanced our home and paid off the majority of any debt. We had one credit card with an unpaid balance of about seven thousand dollars. That was okay because I had taken out some extra money with the refinance just to bank. I knew we could easily pay that one card off if we wanted to and the interest rate was at or close to zero percent.

Both my wife and I were working full-time and were probably going to bring in around ninety thousand together. This was going to be a productive year for us - we would be able to save money which was always a challenge in the past. Prior to this, it seemed for one reason or another only one of us was working full-time, so we stayed at the getting-things-paid level but not doing much more.

My wife began having some issues on her job where she had been employed for seven years. We found out much later the issues related more to her boss and some family matters he was confronting at the time. However, the end result was my wife left her job in January 2006 and the whammy had struck again. Now we found ourselves back in the situation where we had only one full time income. I did not sweat it because we had the money from the refinance. She would find something she wanted to do and we would be back on track. Also, since we were in a better position I could look into some of the money making ideas I had in real estate and the stock market.

One thing I always wanted was to get out of the rat race. I was doing a good job managing the money we had, not even flirting with spending for anything we did not need. One thing I was not going to do was fall back into another situation where I could not easily pay all our bills. My wife got her real estate sales license by April and she began looking for different avenues to put it to work.

Around mid-year my wife came to me with an idea from a seminar she had attended that sparked her interest. Up to this point I was rebuffing everything that was going to cost us any money to start; this was not our first trip down a path like that. We had attended many money making opportunity events together and bought in to several which did not pan out successfully.

The latest one was a company that claimed to be associated with Robert Allen. Robert Allen is a real estate guru who has taught literally thousands of people how to make money in different ways using real estate. I really did not want to hear about it, but after a few days I listened to her talk and we watched the Robert Allen videos on the internet. I got excited about the multiple streams of income. My wife was going to do this herself and I was going to be on the outside for the most part.

We talked to this guy on the phone who all but guaranteed the return of our investment within three months. Even though my internal guidance system was telling me "No! No! No!" I did not pay attention and we shelled out about $11,000.00 with a credit card. My credit was excellent and I could easily carry the balance on a credit card for three months with zero percent interest so we went ahead and my wife got started.

We received a bunch of material in the mail: books, tapes, and all kinds of other materials to get this business going. It was not very long before we found out that this company was no longer associated with Robert Allen, probably due to some shady practices, but they retained the right to use his name and accomplishments to get people in to their system. They preyed on trusting, gullible people like us. We took their bait and there was no way to get our money back. I was livid when I realized what they had done and I let them know it.

After I complained, they sent us another box full of other books, CDs, and materials from the actual Robert Allen program which we could have purchased for about a third of what we had already paid. I was enraged! We were not yet behind the eight ball again, but I wanted to get moving on the right plan to secure our financial future. We had been down this road before, but not to the tune of $11,000.00 and I wanted this to work. The question I should have asked myself is, what if this does not work? What is plan B or C? Much later, I realized that the idea of making a lot of money in real estate sounded like fun to me, it made me feel good just to think about it, and we had not made any money at that moment. The reality that we now had $11,000.00 on a credit card was not fun, and quickly replaced that good feeling of mine. If I had just understood that my thoughts create my reality, I would have stayed focused on what felt good.

CHAPTER **10**

We Can Make This Work

In September 2006 we went to another one of those business seminars with my wife's real estate broker with no intention of buying, just looking. I found a software program that I thought was the missing piece I had been searching for in my stock and option trading. I had used a program about five years before and after losing around nine thousand dollars for the year I just figured it was not going to work for me. I had made money and lost money but at that time I could not chance anymore losses.

This new software program that I found added to what I already knew. I was ready to make a go at it again. I started to practice and prepare for my ultimate easy life where I would pay back the eleven thousand dollars plus the fifteen hundred for the new program and finally get to the financial position I wanted to be in and help others around me do the same.

I worked with the new system not really trying to learn everything about it (that would have been far more information than I needed). I just focused in the area that I felt most important for what I was going to do. For the last three months of 2006 I prepared to take on the stock market again, this time fully equipped to secure the lifestyle I always wanted. I used my Investor's Business Daily subscription, mainly the top 100 list to locate the best stocks. To play my options trades, I used a special protocol to filter the best stocks and find those special few that had the movement, price range, volume range, and a few other key indicators that would always give me the edge. I had set up my new brokerage account with a trader's broker because their format was set up for people like me. I had my financial backing as I stated earlier with over four hundred thousand in unused credit. I was ready to get live in January 2007.

I started the account off with five thousand. I lost a little and won a little but for the most part I was staying about even. I figured that month what I needed was to be online more to watch what was happening during the other parts of the trading day especially the last hour. I was relegated to making my moves early in the morning because I had to be at work by 8:30 am.

I purchased the 8525 phone from Cingular which was supposed to give me access to the internet so I would be able to watch my position and make trades if needed but it was apparent early on that this plan was not going to work. That phone was the top of the line at that time but just did not have the capability to handle the trading platform I was using. That left me in a bit of a bind.

My Dad, at eighty years old, got really sick in mid-January. He was in the hospital for a couple weeks and it was apparent that it was no longer going to work for him to be home alone as he had been. I took a leave of absence from work and spent most of the next three months tending to my Dad during the day. This also allowed me to watch the stock market (cha- ching) at what I thought were those critical times of the day. It worked pretty well at first, but I realized I still had a little learning curve so I worked on that, learning some additional techniques to master options trading.

I also realized a few other things: my account had been restricted, meaning I was being limited on the amount of trades I was able to make. In order to work my system in the manner I wanted, I needed to add more money to my account which was not a problem as long as my system was working decently and I was making money.

I took sixty thousand dollars of credit at zero percent and put that in my account. I could now trade as free as a bird! I say that in jest, because this was not a game to me; it was serious business and I was going to win at this. I noticed some things the market makers would do in the pricing and manipulating of the options I was trading. I had access to level II screens when I traded before so I knew when the bigger traders came in to the picture. I was not using level II now but I had other indicators of the way the market was moving, what blocks of position were backed up, and who was trading them. Sometimes I knew I was being plucked out and scalped so I had to disguise my intentions somewhat and stay in some positions longer than I wanted to, in order to get movement in the direction I wanted. I also took another trading class just to see if there were some tidbits that would give me a greater edge. I did find a couple of good nuggets.

By the time I went back to work it was around mid-May and I was still about even with my system but the potential was good. When I got back to work I was able to set up my computer so I could have my trading platform running in the background where I could periodically look at it to see how things were going. I also had the ability to web-trade a position if needed.

It was the citical, transforming moments from this point in my life which would lead to what now is Applied Freedom Technologies. Many of us go through our day to day existence and in our mind, spirit or somewhere in our being is this little voice saying "something is not right here." Like me, you may have to respond quickly in some critical moments. I am hoping that by sharing my missteps perhaps you will have less of your own. It is possible right now to train your mind to focus on the solution for you to achieve whatever it is that you desire.

CHAPTER 11

Pulling Up the Anchor

My ride to work was longer because of a change in my work position and building, which meant the positions I took in the morning before I left home had to be the right positions because the activity that could occur during an hour in the morning could cause some serious damage to my account. The last hour of the day was even more critical. The market was behaving a lot more erratic than in the past six or seven months. On top of that, I would miss making moves (taking a different position in a trade) to set up for the next day or close out a position that did not look as promising as I previously thought, because of a meeting or something going on in the office at that time.

In July I was able to secure a line of credit on my home of 100k that would cover any losses I sustained. Things were still getting tougher, meaning it was harder for me to get my system on track, the market seemed more erratic than I had ever seen before.

I had another unexpected event happen, I was called in to a meeting with my manager and two region managers and they asked me if I had been visiting a trading site on my computer. I told them yes, I did have a site running in the background and that it did not interfere with me completing my work. They told me my computer was flagged in the top 100 computers in the company with time on a non-business website, which to them meant I was doing non-business activities. It was pretty significant to be flagged in the top 100 since the company had 200,000 plus employees. I really could not blame them or be upset with them because of the circumstantial evidence they had. Even though my work was always completed in a timely matter, they probably thought I would have gotten even more work done if I didn't spend so much time on that website. Needless to say, I believed I was very close to being fired and my ability to view positions at work went to zero.

By the time I was called on the carpet for my non-business internet activity I had lost about fifty-seven thousand, more than my salary for one year. I am sure you have heard of people turning to God when they get in a really bad situation but I was already with God. Now I was having extra sessions with Him almost every night, but honestly I could not put into words the way I felt. It was like my guts were outside of my body and I could only feel the emptiness that was left.

In October I tried making a couple moves to get back on track but the national mortgage melt down was the reason for the erratic market and it did not appear anything I had planned for option trading was going to work.

I told my wife what I had done in either late October or early November. I still get a tightness in my chest, even while typing these words. I had created a mess with no ideas for how to fix it. The fact that I acknowledged that I created this situation was a lot more significant than I knew at that time. I know now that you must accept responsibility in order to be in control of your reality. I still had my equity line for what that was worth, and I still had a place to live. The problem with that was the payments on the equity line were not at zero percent, I used it as a layover or carry-over account. I would pay off one of my credit cards to get the next zero percent card and save on the interest. My credit was still good because I always made my payments on time. At this time some of the payments were pretty steep but I was making it work.

I made some other moves in the market at the end of December and I was able to get a little money back. However, I am the first to admit that my plan to achieve this awesome lifestyle was in the hole about 80 thousand dollars, including commissions.

In January the following year I made a few more moves trying to capitalize on my December momentum. The market was still pretty erratic and my profits were not consistent so I just pulled back from the trading. Now that I had created this mountain of credit card debt I briefly thought about filing bankruptcy but I was too proud and too attached to my good credit rating to do that.

My wife had signed on with a new insurance company and she also had a securities license. She was working her insurance business which was another reason we could not file for bankruptcy. I still had my insurance license and I worked with her part-time. I had let my securities licenses go about three years earlier because I could not find a place to park them (keep them active without using them), so we were both basically working night and day to right this ship. In April, I gave option trading another try and I made over five thousand that month, but gave it back pretty quickly in May. I have not made a live trade since that time. I still like to paper trade - I do not lose any money that way.

CHAPTER **12**

Trying to Stop the Slide

The next bomb shell dropped in June when the bank zipped up our equity line. I had used about 25,000, leaving the remaining 75,000 open and available for me to make credit card swaps when I needed to. The blow from the loss of the equity line really had me scrambling. I had to make something happen. I have never been the type of person to ask for help and the only person I would ask was my Dad, but I knew his situation and he could not help me out of this one.

After a few days of internal battling, I let my pride go and made a call to my friend from our old church, the leader of the men's fellowship. I had not spoken with him in a while and I did not want to call on him asking for something but he was one of the few people I knew who might have the money to help me. I was in need of about one hundred and sixty thousand - I know the numbers because it was devastating to me. I still had money in my brokerage account which was over 30 thousand but that was not even close to offsetting the 160 thousand.

I called my friend and spoke with him but unfortunately the economy had hit his business very hard the year before and he was in a pretty bad financial situation as well. I was glad I had contacted him. Even though he was not able to help me financially it was good to have someone to talk to, and he said he would pull out whatever other resources or contacts he had to help me. I do not remember how many times we spoke over the next year but it was always good to sit down and speak with him; we were actually helping and encouraging one another.

There was one other person I dared to call and this was a very hard call. I met this person as a result of our children attending the same school. It was a private boarding school that we were very fortunate to have both our sons attend. It cost a significant amount of money to go to this school so naturally the parents of most of the students were pretty well off financially.

One day on my lunch break I called one of the fathers I had become acquainted with. I really felt bad, almost like I was committing a crime by calling, but like I said I was truly in a bad position. What if he could help me and I did not call? I could not miss that chance. I had to again put down my pride, deal with the tightness in my stomach and call. He was very nice on the phone; he was apparently on vacation at the time. He did not make me feel bad for calling him and I felt a small sense of relief, not that he was going to help me but because I had done something I never thought I would do. I was still at square one thinking about how I would make this work and how I was going to get us out of the mess I created.

It was around this time that I started seeing advertisements for one of those "better your life" events where people tell you how they have gone from rags to riches and the system they used to do it. For a discounted price you could use their proven system for success and change your life. As I stated before, my wife and I had gone to many of these events during our years together.

At the event, I was already mentally worn down so I found myself buying one of those programs to get me back on the right track. By the time I got it home I was already kicking myself. I will not say I called myself stupid but I probably did. On the last day of the event, I took the product back with the intention of dropping it off and leaving, but since I was there I decided to sit down and listen to what was going on.

As it turned out, the person speaking was none other than Robert Allen – the person whose programs I thought I was buying which got me into this mess to begin with. That is what I told myself anyway. I listened and thought to myself, I have got about one more shot at getting us out of this and I have to go for it. I was already in credit card hell, so I went for it. It cost $30,000 for their premium program, that's right, $30,000.00 –"put it on my credit card, please."

CHAPTER **13**

A New Way Out

Within the next three months my wife and I went to a couple of boot camps, read a lot of material, set up power business contacts in several cities and went through field training in Indianapolis. We had a few deals on the table, some good potential in Atlanta, and we did a lot of work in St. Louis, but for a combination of different reasons we did not pull the trigger on the properties. As it turned out we could have ended up in a worse position (if that was possible) had we proceeded with those deals.

Some may wonder why my wife stayed with me through all of this. We have been through a lot of things together and we have our issues. But one thing we have never wavered on is doing what we feel is best for our sons, giving them the best opportunity for success in whatever they chose to do later in life. These events were taking place when our oldest son had just begun college and our youngest was in his last couple years of high school. We did not want them to have any distractions. Since both of them were away from home it was easier for them to stay focused on their studies; they may have had an inkling something was not right, but nothing to grab on to. As far as they were concerned their parents were solid on all footings and that is the way it has always been.

My parents were divorced when I was very young; I do not know exactly when. My wife had some issues in her family as well and of course that is not unusual. We still had good relationships with our parents for the most part and always got together as a family for the big holidays, but never both sides of the family together. To make a long story bearable we both had to deal with things in our families growing up that we did not like, and we wanted our children to have a different experience. My wife is the best possible mother I could have chosen for our children and if I could have picked a mom other than mine it would be my wife.

In October 2008 I remember sitting in the new church building that we helped to build with our giving. We were still tithers but we gave money above and beyond that. I sat there with about two hundred and twenty five thousand dollars in credit card debt, much of it due to interest and cash advance fees. I sat there saying to myself "Okay God what are you going to do to help me out of this?" For about a month I got no answer.

I remember that on November 30th I was just done. The pressure was too much. My wife was asleep, I went to my bathroom, got down on my knees, and tears came to my eyes as I said to God "If you are out there You need to do something for me now, now!"

Shortly after that, I believe it was on a Saturday morning that I was home alone and depressed. I turned on my computer and a woman started talking about healing yourself. Apparently I had left the CD from our field training in the computer from the night before. On this CD our field training instructor included some self-help websites along with other information that I had no idea was there.

What this lady Carol Tuttle was saying intrigued me so I went to her website. She sparked the start of a change in my perspective in this life. There was a lot of information on her website but the thing that got to me was she said I could relieve my stress in one minute and it would only cost me $3.95. I could not afford much at that moment, but I could handle $3.95 to see what she was talking about. For $3.95, I received an introduction to EFT (Emotional Freedom Technique) or Tapping as it is also called.

EFT was a big step for me in that it allowed me to stop the chatter. You cannot control your thoughts or your body until you have control of your mind. I had so many things going on at that time it was difficult to stop the chatter. EFT was not the only energy tool I learned from Carol Tuttle, but with it I was able to start attracting peace in my mind. Training your mind to focus on the solution starts with controlling your thoughts and we all have the power to do that. The EFT process is not consistent in its application although all applications include tapping on energy centers as mapped out by meridian lines in the body. Carol's process included a forgiveness step, which assisted me in forgiving myself which allowed me to find some peace.

EFT works using the same principle as acupuncture, utilizing the meridian pressure points on the body to relieve stress. I thought that was pretty cool and I started doing the tapping after reading more of her information. Part of Carol's story was that she had also been in serious credit card debt to the tune of $30,000, which was a lot of money, but as you all know by now, I had a lot more than that.

Because the tapping worked so well for me I was open to some of the other energy tools available on Carol's web-site. I was introduced to gem therapy, rapid eye movement, energy magnets, eye patch therapy, and a few other clearing modalities. I was open to just about anything that would keep me in a good state of mind. This was just the beginning; mentally I felt better but the situation I had put myself and my family in was far from resolution.

Carol was also teaching about the law of attraction. I had heard about that before but this seemed a little different. I searched the internet for "law of attraction" and of course there was a lot of information that came up. I was drawn to Bob Doyle and his book, "Wealth beyond Reason."

I read that book a couple of times back to back to make sure I was understanding what I was reading. I started looking at my life in terms of the law of attraction. From what I was reading, I created the situation I was in and more importantly I had the power to change it. After reading Bob Doyle's book, I started thinking more about what I was doing and how my thoughts and actions could be the reason that I was in the situation I was in.

The proverbial light came on for me and I saw very clearly why my prayers seemed to work only some of the time and why some were not answered at all. I knew how to pray, at least I knew what I had been taught and I had faith that God would answer and all that stuff. I understood why the visualizing part of prayer was important and why I needed to see the end result from the beginning. I understood the repetitious process of praying without ceasing.

All these things I had known and used but there were two things in Doyle's book, that for whatever reason I did not know to apply in my prayer process until I understood them clearly in reading his book. They are pretty simple things but would take some practice to do well. 1) Is to bring the physical sensations of all five senses as much as possible, in to what I am trying to visualize, and 2) combine that with a positive feeling of emotion as I saw myself with my answered prayer or visualization.

One other very important message I received from Bob Doyle's book is the belief that I did in fact create my own reality. This was not easy to accept at first, because it meant that I was entirely responsible in the situation I was in no matter how bad it was or what others had contributed. The light I saw at the end of the tunnel from this was that if I created it, I have the power to create over it something better for me and my family.

I began researching more about the law of attraction and the internet was a fabulous assistant - there was a lot of information available. I watched many YouTube videos, and by

January I latched on to Jerry and Esther Hicks. After watching some of the YouTube videos, I went to their website and listened to the introduction to Abraham audio several times. The information I was listening to would be classified in a book store or library as new age (I do not agree with that classification). I listened to this information with earpieces in my ears while working at my desk, then I ordered the five-CD set.

This information was the cutting edge in my eyes; I wondered how I never knew about this before. I wished I had known this before I accumulated so much debt. What really mattered most now was whether this information was accurate. If it were in fact true, than there is a lot of information that has been generally accepted in this world that is not true.

My wife had purchased the book "Money and the Law of Attraction" by Jerry and Esther Hicks. She had the book for about two months and I had not paid much attention to it because she was not reading it. The book was on her nightstand under some other books. I began constantly listening to the CD's, reading the book and implementing the information that I had learned as best I could. I was on full overload because I was not just behind the eight ball - I was barely hanging on to the table.

CHAPTER 14

The Wool Over My Eyes

My wife told me about a man she met who had done a lot of business with loans. Since I had my real estate license, maybe we could work on something together. We met with him and talked about real estate and other ideas and for some reason he started telling us about someone who got his house back by getting his "Strawman." Now I had never heard anything about this before but being someone who always felt that there is more to this life than I was actually seeing, I wanted to know what else was out there.

I met with the man again and we talked more about the loans business he had done and was in the process of doing. At the time he was working on a big deal for an ex-heavyweight boxing champion. We talked more about this Strawman information and I realized that if I could get my Strawman maybe I could own my home free and clear and would have the money to pay off the credit card situation I had created.

I began doing my own research about this and I found out your Strawman is the separate entity which is set up by the system/government for each one of us to transact business in commerce. The United States Corporation has been in bankruptcy since 1933, and the court system, banking system, public works, and the general system of commerce are running under a set of rules I never learned about in school or even knew existed. Could this be the reason some people get ahead in life and most people do not? I started to think maybe this is the reason I am getting my ass kicked in life right now - I do not know the rules of the game.

The first few sites I looked up on the internet about the Strawman and how to get him made me a little leery. First of all, the websites themselves were dark and made to seem sinister, then they said things like you could purchase this do-it-yourself package for $1,500 and the next step up was a package with more information at another cost. The alternative was you could pay five thousand dollars and they would get your Strawman for you.

I did not have five thousand dollars, which I might have paid for a sure thing of getting the title to my home. I continued to search YouTube and follow the threads for all this new information I was attracting and came across an older man named Winston. He was talking about the Strawman and he did not seem shady like the other websites I had gone to. He was straightforward and helped me understand a lot of information that I had already heard with his delivery. He offered several CD's about the Strawman and other areas relating to commerce that we all deal with every day. There was even something there regarding credit card debt, oh boy.

I ordered some of Winston's material and listened to it over and over again while I sat at my desk doing my work. This worked pretty well for me because the information I listened to was either on a CD I brought in or something I downloaded and put on a flash drive. I did not have to think about being flagged for being on the internet again. I worked on getting my Strawman back using Winston's information and coaching calls from one of his representatives. I had not yet spoken directly with Winston, but that would come later.

The information I was learning was hard for me to accept but exciting to hear at the same time. I was a bit baffled by how I could be at this point in my life and not been exposed to this information. I thought I found a treasure chest with the Jerry and Esther Hicks information, the information from Winston was just as intriguing only in relation to our operation in commerce.

Another influential person I listened to a lot is David Childerley of England. I found David on YouTube while looking for more information regarding credit card debt. He was doing this "freeman on the land" segment where he was giving a day-by-day account of his stand for his rights as a human being who was not under the authority of the local government.

I was really interested to see how this was going to work out. David began testing statutory law by not paying parking tickets, not registering his vehicle, not paying certain government taxes and other similar burdens we are all taught that we must do. David was going to provide updates on these situations so we would know the end result, which was either he would be put in jail by the legal system or he would be left alone to live his life as a freeman under common law. Of course I was hoping for the freeman outcome.

David also had a series on YouTube titled "2012 and Beyond" which was very interesting and timely for me because of the information I had been researching at the time. I recall that part seven, the final segment in the series was a complete outline of information with the same conclusions that I had about the financial system in our society. It was all laid out for the world to see.

I could not help but think about how bold this guy was to put this information out even though I agreed with him based on my own research. The way David laid it out made a lot of sense and I believe that if people had a chance to view it, a ground swell revolution was not outside the realm of possibility. I was actually afraid for him, as he was calling a lot of powerful people on the carpet, not by name but by position, in significant areas in the structure of our society. David lived in England but the similarity to America could easily be seen.

As it turned out, the final segment of the series was only viewable online for a short period of time. I do not even think it was up more than a day or so. I do know that after I accessed it the first time it was not available twenty-four hours later.

David still has a lot of information available online related to tapping, self-healing, and self-empowerment. Part of my morning ritual is to listen to his "Tapping to Empower Yourself" coaching videos.

The first interview I completed for my own website was with David. I spoke with him regarding his life, the things he has done and part seven of his "2012 and Beyond" segment.

There is one other person I found on the internet whose systems and processes I made a regular part of my methods to stay focused and positive and he goes simply by "Rama". Rama created body activation processes which are unlike anything else I had come across. I had come across many different ideas and methods that assist in mental and physical enhancement and there were really only a few that I adopted. Rama's processes are unique and I used them because they work.

CHAPTER **15**

I Do Not Really Owe Money on My Credit Cards?

Mary Elizabeth Croft was another person who garnered my attention. Her book, "How I Clobbered Every Bureaucratic Cash-Confiscatory Agency Known to Man" caused me to think that maybe there is another way for me to get out of this credit card situation.

Mary wrote about her real life encounters with issues regarding debt. She is a pioneer and paved the way for people like me to learn the truth as it relates to credit card debt and much more. As I stated before, I never felt right about how our society operates, (meaning some things just did not seem fair) but I was not able to put a finger on what felt out of place.

I found Mary Croft through another website during my research. When I located what I believed to be a website with good, legitimate information (meaning there was something in the information that resonated with me, so I made a choice to accept it until I had Proof of it to be inaccurate) I went with the flow of the stream. If there were links to other websites or individuals I would follow the links, review the information, measure how it felt in my spirit, and then move on.

I found a site called "Get out of Debt Free" and that was something that sounded very good to me at the time. Around April that year I got served with my first lawsuit by an attorney that claimed to represent a major bank/credit card company. That may have been true but I did not bow down to them, so they sold it off to a debt-buying attorney; this is what I believed from what I had learned so far.

A few months earlier, around the beginning of that year I could no longer handle making the credit card payments on all the outstanding accounts so I was doing what I could, as best I could. It was not enough and I began receiving many calls from credit card companies regarding my delinquent accounts.

The thought of filing bankruptcy was at the front of my mind again, but it took another couple of months before I decided to move in that direction. I met with several attorneys before making a deposit and caving in.

Once I made that decision I did feel a release of pressure even though the process was far from over. One benefit was that I got the credit card companies to stop calling me. I would just direct them to my attorney and that was that, no more calls from them.

The cost for the bankruptcy was about $3,300.00 and our deposit was $500.00. They would not file the case until they had most or all of the money so we were on a monthly installment plan. I was no longer being harassed by the credit card companies. I still had the pending lawsuit but they had also backed off so I continued to look for another way out of that situation.

The "Get out of Debt Free" website was great; it confirmed the information I had learned from my prior research, which was that I did not owe the credit card companies any money. If I really did not owe the credit card companies anything then surely I did not owe the collection companies and debt buyers anything.

Apparently, after 3-6 months of nonpayment, the credit card companies write-off your account as bad debt, and turn the account over to internal or external collections. They basically sell your debt to the highest bidder and get your account off their books.

Once the collection companies get the account, they start their own process of trying to get you to acknowledge that a debt is owed. If you do that, then they claim to represent the credit card company and try to get you to agree and pay some portion of whatever the balance was on the account, but remember the credit card company has already written off the amount as bad debt, so why give them anything?

CHAPTER **16**

Oh You Are Going to Pay

I will call this the **second wave assault**. I believe it must depend at least in part on what they (collection companies) see as the balance on the account as to whether they will continue to pursue you if you do not give in to their harassing collection calls. There must be some kind of cost-benefit formula they use.

If they get you to agree that you owe the money or some money and you will pay them then it is good they bought the account. They will make more money than they spent with very little effort and they are happy. You will probably pay less than you allegedly owe and the situation will be done.

But more than likely if you did not pay the credit card company because you did not have the money, you will not pay these guys either, so they may try a few other scare tactics before they sell your debt to the next collection agency. This may happen two or three times before your account ends up being bought for (I am only guessing) pennies on the dollar by some debt-buying attorney. In my opinion this is where attorneys have earned their reputation as snakes.

When dealing with credit card debt, you can expedite the process of having most credit card companies write off your account. This will not clear your credit report but it may buy you some additional time to resolve your situation, or if you are lucky you may not be pursued by your particular credit card company.

I found several websites that have a process outlined for you to send the credit card company a letter requesting them to verify the debt they say you owe. The process can be done with one letter, or as in my case, I used a three step process. "Get out of Debt Free" gave me access to templates for the letters and made the process pretty simple, but it was time consuming for me because I had so many accounts to deal with.

Most of the sites where you find sample letters have a disclaimer that you are using them at your own risk or they are for entertainment purposes only. Everyone, especially those who try to assist people like me who were in a bad situation must also protect themselves.

The purpose of the letters is for the creditors to validate the debt they say you owe. As a human being you have rights under common law or **The Uniform Commercial Code.** When you exert those rights, the opposing party, in this case the credit card companies, will usually never respond to the letters requesting validation of the debt, because a human being cannot contract with an entity like a credit card company or any of the other companies you typically pay bills to. The reason for this ties back to the Strawman we talked about a little earlier. Also the under the **Bills of exchange act 1882: "You cannot sell debt that has already been paid off"** so once your debt has been written off that should be the end of that account **(UCC)**.

I believe all the credit card companies I sent these letters to eventually wrote off the accounts as bad debt, if they had not already done so. One company responded to my letters but did not validate the debt under the Uniform Commercial Code.

The third letter in the series establishes a tacit agreement by their non-response that they were not owed any debt and would not pursue the matter any further. The credit card companies wrote off the debt and sold it to a collection company in most cases.

There were two credit card companies that did not sell the accounts, but they were still written off as bad debt.

Then I began receiving letters and phone calls from different companies claiming I now owed them the debt or balance for that particular account. The "Get out Of Debt Free" website gave me template letters for credit card companies and collection agencies. The next step in the process for me was sending the letters to the collection companies. There is a different set of letters for dealing with collection companies; they have even less standing under common law.

I sent a request for validation of the debt to the collection companies and in most cases I would not hear from the company again. Sometime later I would receive a letter from another collection company claiming I owed them money on the same account.

My take is simply this: I really do not owe the debt, because the debt has already been paid. However if you accept the debt as yours by any form of acknowledgement then the collection company will take the money you give them. When you see how the credit card system is designed to keep you in debt and take advantage of you, you will not have any issue with playing their game, knowing and using their rules. It seems that if it will cost them more than a letter or a few phone calls it is not worth the effort for them because they cannot prove you owe the money.

The essence of your letter to the collection agency is this (1) You are asking for validation of the debt (the actual accounting), (2) Verification of their claim against you, a sworn affidavit or a hand-signed invoice in accordance with the Uniform Commercial Code, and (3) A copy of the contract signed by both parties [and therefore binding on both parties]. Under common law in order to contract, there are certain basic elements which must be met, and your credit card agreement does not meet them. This is known by the credit card and collection agencies.

I had two problems with the letter process, but they were not related to the letters. The letters appeared to work well for me. My issue was I had so many different accounts with large balances that eventually the debt would be bought by one of those debt-buying attorneys. Those attorneys really are not concerned with common law because the justice system is stacked in favor of the courts, and they are officers of the court. Once they get you in your local court, especially if you live in a metropolitan area, you will be tricked or coerced into their court process which is not under common law. I will get back to that in a moment.

Unfortunately for me, how to deal with debt-buying attorneys was not covered on the "Get out of Debt Free" website when I was using their services. Fighting against the debt-buying attorneys in court proved to be a challenge which was more difficult for me to overcome. I attempted, as many other people have tried before me, to go before the court and not accept responsibility for the actions of my Strawman.

It could be that I did not have enough information, but I certainly did not want to end up in jail for any length of time, so I had to respond to the debt-buying attorneys. I am sure I would have gotten out of jail, but I did not want to go in at all. When the debt-buying attorneys sue you claiming you still own this credit card debt that has been written off and sold, you still have to respond - at least I did.

I did attempt to claim my common law rights, but once you appear in court (and acknowledge your name) you will not be under "the law of the land" you will be under admiralty law which is the "law of the sea" even though you will be standing on dry land.

The letters worked well for the debt-buying attorneys who were in other states, but for the local scavenger, I mean local debt-buying attorneys, they were undaunted by the letters.

One attorney who filed a suit against us actually fabricated the proof of service of the lawsuit. We received a judgment and never had the opportunity to defend against the claim. It took a lot of footwork and brainwork to learn the rules of the system to get that judgment set aside, but I was able to do it.

CHAPTER 17

I Am Okay No Matter What Happens, Everyone Is Okay No Matter What Happens

By September 2009 I had exerted a lot of effort toward understanding and working the law of attraction information I received, especially as it relates to the Jerry, Esther, and Abraham material.

I read their *Money and the Law of Attraction* material over and over. I listened to the CD set I purchased over and over. I believed the information I was receiving was real and if I had in fact created this situation for myself then I could get myself out of it.

I used the principles I was learning on simple things like traffic and it worked for me. The distance I drove to and from work every day was the same but I hardly ever got caught in traffic anymore. I set my intention once I got into my car in the morning for safety and a smooth, easy-flowing ride and that is what I got almost every day. I would pre-pave situations throughout my day (pre-paving is basically setting up in your mind what you want from a situation before you enter the situation). If there was a meeting I was going to attend I would set my intention for what I wanted to take place and things would turn out well for me.

I used what I learned to make changes in my life, but there was one thing that bothered me regarding the law of attraction. I had a question which I never heard a response to, the question of being filled with the Holy Spirit and speaking in other tongues. I had done a bit of searching but had not found an answer to that question.

As I mentioned earlier, I had grown up in church, and early on I was taught that speaking with tongues was something weird or bad. Once I had made a decision to learn about the Bible from the best teachers I could find, I gained an understanding of how to use it and live by it. There also came a better understanding of the infilling of the Holy Spirit which was one of the most powerful experiences I have ever had in my life.

Jerry and Esther Hicks, along with Abraham Hicks were having a live workshop coming up in the Los Angeles area. I signed up for it over a month in advance. It was set for September 5th and I had made up my mind that I was going to get an answer to my question. I had not been to one of these workshops before but I knew there would be three to four hundred people attending and very few are chosen to go up to what is called 'the hot seat' to ask Abraham a question. By the time I got there on that Saturday I knew I would be the first one called on because I had set my intention with such clarity.

I had made a mistake though; my intention was not focused so much on getting my question answered, as it was in not having the question avoided (talked around and not answered). The answer made sense but was not absolutely complete, which was my fault. I should have asked a few more detailed follow up questions. However this being my first time at one of these workshops, and being the first one called, I really was not aware that I could do that. The fact that my question was not in the slightest way avoided was enough encouragement for me to move forward full force in practicing the law of attraction, and that is what I did.

CHAPTER **18**

It Was Self Defense or Defending Myself?

It was after I attended Abraham Hicks' workshop that I began sending those letters to the credit card companies, collection companies and debt-buying attorneys. There were also a few other things I was working on simultaneously. I was preparing to take on the one law suit that had already been filed against me. I worked every angle I could find. I had several coaching calls with Winston who is knowledgeable when it comes to operating in commerce and dealing with the courts. Many of the things he told me to do did not work, but enough of it did work, which showed me that he knew what he was talking about. The reason some of the things I was attempting to do did not work is because the courts will change their own rules and ignore their own rules. I have firsthand experience with them doing that.

I fought with debt-buying attorneys in the courts on a few different lawsuits for almost two years. It was rough going most of the time. It was like having two jobs - my regular job and then the job of representing myself in court. The latter was a lot more work, because there were so many things that needed to be reviewed and completed.

It finally dawned on me that fighting was the reason why I was still dealing with the situation. I had used the law of attraction in other areas in my life and those areas improved. I used the law of attraction with these cases as well, but I had kept up the fight because what they were doing was wrong and I wanted to prove it by winning. I was not winning, so I stopped fighting and began to focus my attention on what I truly wanted. I actually did want to beat those debt-buyers in court, but it is their court and their rules, and under the law of attraction I could fight with them forever. What I truly wanted was for the situation to go away.

I made some other decisions in that area and it took more time. I also took on more damage from the mental wear and tear on the course I had already laid. I was sharpening my skills in the law of attraction arena. At the same time I was working on the lawsuits I was also working on getting control of my Strawman and getting out from under what I was convinced was a fraudulent mortgage.

The process for addressing the credit cards, the Strawman, and what I learned about operating in commerce was a lot to work with at one time. I did not want to wear so many hats at once, but the information seemed valid and was confirmed by several sources, which encouraged me to go a little deeper.

CHAPTER **19**

I Want Control of My Strawman

If by completing the process I could gain control of my Strawman, I thought that would give me back my life in the commerce area. I was already working the "I create my own reality" law of attraction side of the situation but I thought this would make things better faster.

One of the great things about gaining control of the Strawman is with that in place I could own my home free and clear with no more mortgage payments, which was a big motivation for me. It took a lot of work, but once I had the foundation in place I started sending notarized letters and documentation off to the mortgage company. This was supposed to be an administrative process, but if you did not get the desired result then you would have to go to court and resolve it from that angle.

After six or seven months of getting all the documents in order and sending them off to the bank, I received a lot of responses but none of them were the responses I was expecting. At this time I was still dealing with some of the credit card account debt-buyers in court and I was pretty worn down from that. By that time I learned that the court system is not the friendliest place to be if you represent yourself, so I really did not want to go that route with the bank/mortgage company if I did not have to.

Around this time I found out that Winston was going to have a live seminar and one of the primary topics to be discussed was "What really happens when you purchase your home." It was going to address how to get your home back from the bank which was something I had been trying to resolve for the past six months. It was a challenging administrative process, so the information would be helpful.

The seminar provided some very interesting inside information about what has been happening in the mortgage industry for a very long time. The information we received still eludes the vast majority of people who work within the industry not to mention all the homebuyers. The fractional banking system is being used on your mortgage the same way it is used for other deposits on hand by your bank. We learned that in most cases, this means that when you sign a note for $300k (for example), the bank uses your signature to create an additional $900k for a total debt creation of $1.2 million. We saw documents that proved the banks did this.

We were given a lot of information about the acts that are committed against the public at large, usually during the process of buying a home. We also received information about how to get your home back. The seminar fell short in my opinion, because we were not given enough information about how to get it done. I had already done most of the steps that were covered but I was not the expert. When the offer was presented to have an expert complete the process for you, I took what little money I had left at this point and paid to have this process completed for me.

My major setback while trying to do the process myself was, I was not able to get the documents (which were made valid by the mortgage company's tacit agreement) recorded at the county recorder's office in the metropolitan area where I lived. I found it extremely difficult to get anything recorded. I encountered this problem while trying to gain control of my Strawman as well. Whoever put this system together made the nuts and bolts pretty tight, at least in my area of the country. The good news was that the expert assured me there was a way to get the documents recorded in the county recorder's office area where we lived and he had done it in this area in the past, so with that I was ready to go.

CHAPTER **20**

Nothing Like Having Everything on the Line

Once we paid our money, it was supposed to take forty-five to sixty days at the maximum, but the process did not go as planned. The expert we were dealing with was evasive and very difficult to get in contact with. I don't know whether this was a sham to begin with or if the rules of the game changed. I suspect it was the latter. Whatever the reason was, the process was not working for us. The debt-buying attorneys were on our back with case after case and the mortgage company was on us in full assault mode. Now I was almost out of options and it was a question of filing for bankruptcy or losing everything. We decided to file chapter 13 in order to keep our home.

Earlier in the year I went to trial on the first credit card law suit and I fully expected to win, however the judge paid no attention at all to my argument and just ruled in favor of the debt-buyer. The really bad part about that whole thing is that the debt-buying attorney never showed up once. I had to show up a number of times in the case and the debt-buying attorney just sent a show-up attorney who knew nothing about the case.

After the attorney won the case he levied my bank account. Fortunately for me he only went to one bank. It truly felt like my life was being ripped out from under me. It was hard to believe that a stranger can use the system to completely ruin your life. In essence, that is what happened. They levied one of my accounts but they could have gone after all of them. Next they were going to garnish my wages from work. It is not that I had much money in the accounts; it is the principle that bothered me. I tried to figure out a way to stop this from happening and I filed an exemption on the levy.

I was really beyond tired at this point. I would have to stop using banks which was a complete nightmare. From the outside, my wife and I were on a very thin line from extreme disaster. **On the inside I was firm in my belief that the universal laws were real and the primary law was the law of attraction. With that law, I had created this situation, so I could create something different for myself**. (www.myaft.net)

I was due in court in October for the exemption I had filed on the levy. My wife was due in court the same day on another debt-buyer credit card suit, and at the end of the week our house was scheduled to be sold at a trustee sale outside the court.

We did not want to go with our original bankruptcy attorney because we began to feel more like a number rather than people, so we had to find someone else. This was not an easy process because we were really down to the wire. I really had expected the guy working on the mortgage to come through for us until he told me about a week or so before that his process does not stop a foreclosure, which is not what he had previously said.

The attorney we found filed the bankruptcy electronically the day before we were due in court, which was actually a holiday. The courts in my area take every holiday off. We went into court the next day and everything was stayed (meaning it was put on hold). It was not a surprise that the debt-buying attorney for my case did not show up for the levy hearing. As I stated before, he never showed up for anything regarding that case.

However the debt-buying attorney on my wife's case did show up, she was actually one of the partners. She was pissed and apparently came for battle. She asked the judge how it was possible to file a bankruptcy case on a holiday. Even though I did not want to file the bankruptcy, I was still pretty satisfied on the inside that they were pissed. Attorneys, more than the collection companies, do not expect people to fight them and do not want to spend any money. I know I made them spend a lot more time and money than they wanted and they got nothing for it.

CHAPTER **21**

Nothing About This Process Was Easy

There were a few issues with the chapter 13 which extended the time before it was confirmed. It was not actually confirmed until the middle of the following year which is not what we anticipated based on what we knew. The situation we were in was looking bleaker up to the time we filed for bankruptcy, and even afterward, there always seemed to be some little T's that were not crossed. I was steadfast in the belief and practice that I created and controlled my own reality. **I believed the delays we encountered were there to give the Universal powers that be the time to orchestrate this situation in a manner that would be best for me.** (www.myaft.net)

I did a lot of research before I made the decision to go down this path, I did not take it lightly in any way. The information I found about the law of attraction was validated to a point where I was confident it was accurate. I can change my thinking and thereby change my situation and so can anyone else. Prior to accepting this I was being overwhelmed by the situation but now I was using the tools which I had learned and was still learning to ensure that anyone having anything to do with my situation from this point forward would be acting in my best interest. I set my intention to have all things work for my best interest. I cannot say it worked out for me in every situation or even in my timing, but it was working pretty damn well for the most part. I was getting better at using these tools and new knowledge all the time.

This may sound a little outlandish as you read it. I can assure you it was really tough for us as we were going through it and the key word is through it. Once I sold out to the Abraham Hick's material especially the universal law of attraction, knowing these laws work gave me courage to stand my ground by using my thoughts to recreate my situation. Being in control of my thoughts did not mean I was in control of everything around me. But it did mean the result of this situation was going to match my new intention. When I talk about training your mind to focus on the solution, the solution is the intention you set for yourself.

We continued to follow up with the expert who was supposedly still on the job of securing the title to our home. We had expected to receive the title while we were dealing with the chapter 13 filing. It was not until mid-year in 2011 that the person who was supposed to complete the title process for us put it back in our court and I mean that literally. They said we would have to go to court to get it done so we let the situation go and lost the money that we paid for this service. We let the situation go because we decided to let the creation of our new reality take shape and in order to do that we had to let go of the old things.

It was still a big effort to keep our monthly budget on track especially with the planned payment to the chapter 13 trustee every month. If and when we did start to make more money we were concerned that every year the chapter 13 trustee would come in and increase the amount of the planned payment. In early 2012 we had a talk with a very influential person in our life who told us we should not be in a chapter 13. We thought it was the only way to keep our home, and he assured us that this was not the case. So we took his advice and had the chapter 13 converted to a chapter 7. This was also a process that should have taken a couple of months but ended up taking about eight months to complete. **As before, I chalked this up to the universe coordinating activities to provide the best result for us.**

We were also told we should apply for a home modification at the same time as the conversion so they would work hand in hand. It is interesting to note that the attorney who we used for the chapter 13 was not happy that we wanted to have it converted to a chapter 7. We still do not understand why. One thing that he told me was that we got a sweet deal on the chapter 13. He would not sign off on the substitution of attorney so we had to move forward without it.

We were a couple of months in to trying to get the chapter 7 conversion when I received an e-mail from the first attorney saying I should have our new attorney submit the form that he would not sign initially because he was still receiving information regarding our conversion and the modification. He also said we did not need to pay to have the conversion to the chapter 7, and belittled our conversion attorney. I thought it interesting that he told us we did not need to pay again to have the case converted. When we asked him to do it for us he was not willing to do it. He also said we should get the modification done first, and then convert. I was told by others it should be a simultaneous process.

It seems we had a challenge in communicating with both our bankruptcy attorneys. We thought we were just trying to stay on top of our case, they seemed to think we did not need to know what was going on and that we were taking up too much of their time.

I will take the blame for most of this as it was probably due to me or I should say my vibration. One of the things I had heard but certainly have a better understanding of now is how we as human beings communicate by our vibration. Because of what I had to go through in battling those debt-buying attorneys, I really had a sour taste in my month when it came to any attorneys. Even though these were not the debt-buying attorneys I had issues with, the trickery used in the court system is something they all participate in. I actually had to do a lot of work on myself to come to peace with that issue. The tools that I used to do that are the tools you receive in Applied Freedom Technologies.

As things worked out we did not receive approval for the loan modification until August. The chapter 7 conversion should have been completed in April or before, but there were some issues with the conversion attorney which were similar to the chapter 13 attorney. It was difficult to communicate and obtain information regarding what was going on with both cases which was very frustrating.

I do not know whether our conversion attorney dropped the ball at some point or if the courts dropped it but in June, almost five months after we filed for the conversion we received a notice from the chapter 13 trustee that the chapter 13 was being submitted for dismissal not discharge. Dismissal!

All this time we had been asking our attorney what was going on when we could reach him, and now the chapter 13 was about to be dismissed without the conversion in place. Once we got a hold of our conversion attorney and told him, he got in touch with the court and they told him to resubmit the conversion documents. After he did that we had our creditor meeting, the 341 scheduled within a week. **Again I personally attribute these delays to the universal powers that are in control setting and arranging the order of things so that they work for my best benefit**. (www.myaft.net)

The heart shaking and difficult part of this for me was in feeling like these situations took us all the way to the edge mentally, psychologically, and physiologically. It always seemed like the universe was teaching me to expand my faith to the nth degree over and over again. The first few times I was thinking "Okay when I finally tell my story or teach what I have learned, there will be no wondering about what would have happened, I can tell exactly what happened because I was not allowed to get off the ride early."

One thing this did for me was make me mentally tougher and it turns out I needed that mental toughness more than ever in writing this book. I spend so much time as I am writing this thinking "Is this really going to help people in some way, or will they just think I am an idiot?"

The next situation to take me to the edge was the 341 meeting for the chapter 7 conversion. I so badly wanted this completed without having to explain how we ended up with so much credit card debt. We had no other debt, just credit cards and I felt guilty about it, like I was a bad person because of it. I knew that I was responsible for it but I just wanted it to be over, and the day of the 341 meeting was going to be that day; that was my plan.

The meeting was in the same building we went to for the first 341 meeting, but in a different room. We sat there waiting for our attorney, who did not show up and didn't tell us that another attorney would be representing him. It would have been nice to have our actual attorney with us in this meeting.

For the first time we saw all the documentation that was submitted for the chapter 7 conversion. We watched people go up and take their place as their case was called, paying close attention to what was being done so our case would be a simple open and shut.

I did not expect to see any creditors. There were none at the first meeting and from what I had seen practically all the debt had been sold off several times and was now in the hands of who I would call debt wasteland.

When we were called it was confirmed that no creditors showed up. We were going through the process smooth and easy until right at the end I was asked a question. I either did not hear it correctly or was just very nervous and misinterpreted the question that turned the complete hearing upside down. We would not be walking out of there free and clear of our credit card debt.

The question I was told he asked was "What amount of money, if any you do you have on credit cards in the past twelve months?" or something like that. My answer to that should have been "Zero" because we had not used any credit cards for over the past three years. However, the answer I gave after fumbling around with the question a few times was a pretty large number. I thought he was asking what our average balance was the last year we used credit cards. Well with the answer I gave him he wanted a written summary of how we ended up with so much debt. The exact thing I did not want to have to do was staring me right in the face.

Now on that day, more than most days, I had set my intention so that I was the creator of my reality. I did not want to go to the edge anymore. I believed that after that day I would be able to tell the story of how Applied Freedom Technologies had changed my situation completely from being over $260K in debt and devastated to where I could at least breathe again without that burden on my back, but that is not what happened that day.

Instead I found myself pushed to the edge again. It took me about a day and a half to complete the summary. The Trustee had set the continuance of the meeting two weeks out. He also said if the summary was sufficient for him we would not have to come back to continue the hearing.

I sent the summary to our attorney; he would submit it in the proper format. I followed up with our attorney for almost the entire two weeks to see if the summary was submitted to the Trustee. On the day of the meeting my attorney called early and said the Trustee did not have time to review the summary and set another date. It was in another two or three weeks.

I contacted our attorney several times for status but he would not return my calls. We were on edge the whole time. On a Thursday, the day before the meeting, I texted the attorney again. Texting was about the only way I was able to get a response from him and those were still few and far between. But he responded this morning saying the Trustee had accepted my summary, which was great news for me. I asked him when he found out and he said on that Monday. I asked him when he was planning to let us know, and he copped an attitude. I thought to myself, well I will not say what I thought to myself. I just thanked him for his help in this matter and was glad that this was finally done.

It looked as if we would now be able to get our family finances in some sort of decent order. The trial payment process for the modification was to start that month and would be complete in November. From there we could start to rebuild a foundation.

CHAPTER **22**

Things Are Really Getting Better. Aren't They?

My wife closed on a real estate transaction that she had been working on for almost two years and there were a few more in the works. It would not have been good for those to close before the chapter 7 conversion was complete. If we had still been in chapter 13 we would have been in trouble. In chapter 13, on the first of the year it is required for you to send in a financial income statement, and if you show additional income, they will probably require you to pay more whether you could actually afford to or not.

Well what could happen next? I was on vacation from my job at the end of September and the first week of October. Not remembering I was scheduled off for another day I showed up for work on that Monday. The first person I saw as I was walking in was my supervisor who told me he was not expecting me in that night, and playfully I said "Well I will just go back home."

I went into the office fully intending to stay because I was already there, then several other people mentioned to me that

I had the day/night off. This seemed kind of strange to me because Monday is always the busiest night of the week. I thought they would be happy to see me there, but when I said I would just take the day off another time later in the month there was only silence.

The night went on and it turned out to be a pretty light night for a Monday, so that was good. There was something else interesting though. As I was out in the hub doing my normal routine, a supervisor asked me what they were going to do with me. I did not know what he was talking about, so I said I had not heard anything, and asked if he heard anything. He mentioned something that did not relate to me, so I went on about my business.

The next night, one of the guys who was not in the office on Monday (another reason they should have been happy I was there that night), was clearly upset about something which continued into Wednesday night. On Wednesday I asked my supervisor what he had done to make the guy so upset. He said he had not done anything, but something had been done.

Throughout that night and the rest of the week I heard different things but no one said anything to me. I spoke with my manager and supervisor every night and they did not act normal but they did not share any information with me either.

Early Saturday morning maybe around 4:00 a.m., (I normally get off at 7:30 a.m.), one of the drivers came to the window. He was a good guy, talkative as usual, and said to me among other things, "What are they doing with you?" My supervisor and a couple others were in the office, and everyone else in the building was pretty much gone by that time on a Saturday morning. So after the guy left, my supervisor asked me if any-one had talked to me (I had been there the entire week at this point). I said "No, what is going on?" and he said he could not talk about it; he would have our manager talk to me.

Apparently during the week I was on vacation a team from Human Resources had come in and told everyone that some of the positions in the office were going away. I did not know whether I was affected or not but I expected my position to be one that would be eliminated.

I had just come through all this other stuff and now with the final trial payment due for the modification I could be looking at another financial situation. I was not going back to the edge, worrying about how things were going to turn out. I had been through enough; I decided I was not going to freak out or panic anymore. With what I had gone through in the past few years testing the universal laws and proving tools that keep negative thoughts out and cultivating the thoughts that are in line with what I want in my life, I was having good results.

I simply settled in my mind what I used to say and hear when I was going to church on a regular basis: "God is my source, everything else is a resource." The company I worked for was a resource. Now I would look at the universe as my source. I created my reality in the physical time/space reality by my deliberate thought and I would use my internal guidance and listen for the directions I should follow and what actions I needed to take.

I had known what I wanted to do with my life for some time; now it was time to get it done. "The universe provides for me abundantly in all areas and aspects of the physical time/space reality that I choose and want for self, this or something better" is now my mantra.

I had been telling certain people that I did not plan on being at my job much longer. My new manager who had been there a month or so, asked me about working in another position in the office. I knew it would take six to eight months to become proficient in that position so I just told him and everyone else in the office at that time I only planned on being there another year at most.

All the positions in that department were very stress-filled, especially because the company, for whatever reason, would not staff our shift properly. Since I do not like people yelling at me, I might have had to hurt somebody if I took that other office position.

My manager was the third manager of the department in the last fifteen months and the department was not even close to meeting its goals for production. I believe the measurements were not attainable under the current working conditions. There were a lot of people under stress in that department and the direction the company was going in would probably make things even worse. I looked forward to getting out of there.

On the night I found out about the impending changes I had a lot of tension; it felt like pressure in my stomach as I tried to sleep. This was actually the same feeling I had during almost every night at work at the super busy time. I used the tools that I had learned over the prior two years to manage the situation. Had it not been for these tools I do not know how this would have worked out. What I do know is that the tools from Applied Freedom Technologies worked well for me and will work for anyone.

When I woke up the next morning, my inner voice or source told me not to go back to work. I called in sick for a couple of days before going to see my doctor. My body was still showing signs of stress, but the universe was directing my path in the manner I had set with my intention.

My doctor took me out of work for a month. I called to let my manager know and he never called me back. Two days prior when I had called in sick he wanted to know what my symptoms were and told me they needed me back in the office. I guess his caring stopped when my doctor took me out of work. Just to be fair, I never heard from anyone else in my department during the time I was off work. I did have a human resources person call. They did not ask how I was doing; they called to tell me my position had been eliminated and there were no full time positions available for me at that time.

My primary goals became getting this book completed and having my introductory seminar for the Applied Freedom Technologies coaching courses up and running. Assisting others in learning from my experiences will be a major part of my chosen lifestyle. I am determined to use what I have learned to teach others. We all have the power to create the life we want; the proof is in these pages.

CHAPTER **23**

Credit Card Master Attractor

I am going to review as plainly and with as much detail as I can recall another situation in my life where the law of attraction was identifiably in action. The most obvious situation was in my credit card accumulation. As I mentioned before, I received my first credit card at age seventeen. I was not so interested in other credit cards and I rarely used the one I had. It felt good to have that gold card by American Express, the only gold card on the market at that time.

It was not my intention to start collecting credit cards. The credit card companies began sending me more and more credit card offers. I am sure it was because I kept a good credit score and always paid my credit cards on time. I was offered credit cards from banks and financial institutions as well as from every major gasoline company, department stores, furniture stores, and most any store I went into. At some point I just started sending in the applications and then it seemed I received even more offers. I would never pay an annual fee to keep any of the credit cards - not even the department store or gasoline cards. The only card I paid a fee for was my first

American Express Gold card, and I had that fee waived more than once over the years.

At some point I realized that I had over four hundred thousand dollars when I combined the credit card limits, and that amount did not include the department store and gasoline cards. The height of this credit card collecting for me was around 2003. Then I started receiving cash advance checks from my credit card companies. The checks started out at maybe five thousand or two thousand, and usually I got them at zero percent for six months, eight months or even fifteen months. Sometimes my interest rate was .09% and sometimes there was a cash advance fee, sometimes I got the fee waved.

I started playing this credit card game not really thinking much of it. I deposited the checks in my bank account. I liked to have big dollars in my accounts; the people at the banks treat you better. I already knew that from working all those years in the family business. We dealt with a lot of money on a weekly basis and a thirty thousand dollar payroll at the end of the week was standard procedure.

I knew it was the teller's job when they saw a certain amount of money just sitting in your savings or checking account to try and get you over to their financial person. I liked that kind of attention. It also just felt good to have money in my account. Even though I did not really understand the law of attraction then, I was still trying to incorporate it in some way.

As I paid off the ten thousand from this card or that card, the checks started to get larger. I would get cash advance checks for twenty thousand, twenty-five thousand and still at zero percent interest or close to it. At some point, a year or two into doing this, the banks, finance and other credit card companies started to buy each other out. I did not like this at first because I thought the right hand would start to figure out what the left hand was doing, and somehow what I was doing would not work anymore.

But what actually happened was I ended up with two or three, sometimes even four credit card accounts with the same company. By this point I had already come to the conclusion that I did not have to wait for them to send me the cash advance checks anymore. I could just call them on the phone in most cases and still get the zero percent interest rate.

The other thing that happened as a result of the buyouts and having multiple credit cards with the same company was I could move my credit card limits from one card to another. That was "sweet". I shopped my own credit cards for the lowest interest rate, always looking for zero. I moved most of my limits to that card and kept on rolling it. It was easy to keep my credit card game going because I had so many cards.

I had put a lot of time and effort into credit cards and the universe by the law of attraction was going to give me more of what apparently I wanted. I was given a new position at work, in the same office but on the accounting side. One of my responsibilities was to monitor the Visa credit card activity for all the corporate cardholders in the district where I worked. Anyone who had a card or wanted to get a card would be coming through me.

At the end of each month everyone would send their receipts in a nice package to me. If anyone wanted an increase in their Visa Card limit they would have to go through me. That was not my only assignment; it was just a part of what I was there to do.

This was absolutely the law of attraction at work and it gets even clearer. Once I was promoted to that position, I saw changes taking place in other departments. I thought the changes were an abreaction, but I soon learned it was a constant occurrence. Since I was going on my fourth year in that office it was not surprising for me to see some change come my way.

There was a process of downsizing taking place. To make a long story bearable I was chosen to be one of four people to take a lateral move from the district office to the regional office. My primary assignment in this new role was to be the Visa Card liaison for the entire region which at that time included about nine districts in six states. I believe the law of attraction was in full swing as far as bringing me all the activity I could want with credit cards, but that was not the end of it. I was also given the responsibility of working with the managers and supervisors who had American Express Cards throughout the region. I later became the primary backup for the person who worked with the employees who had the American Express Card.

All of this was happening while I was buried almost literally in credit card debt, sending out the letters I talked about earlier to credit card and collection companies, and fighting the credit card lawsuits. The law of attraction really was working well for me. Even though I had not known what I was setting up for myself at the time, I started the ball rolling.

This fact led me to state what I now know to be the truth regarding the law of attraction. Like gravity, it works whether you are consciously aware of it or not. In other words it was working on me by default. There is no way I would have consciously brought this situation upon myself.

I have another example of how my attention to credit cards caused the law of attraction to give me more of what I was giving my attention to. About two years into my regional position at work I was also given the assignment of working with Comdata cards, which are gasoline cards. Initially there was another person in the group taking care of this task, but for some reason it was split. Now I was also responsible for the Comdata cards for half the region and I was the primary backup for the other half.

Once I began to understand the law of attraction, I understood that I created this situation because I create my own reality by my deliberate thought or by default. I started to change my thinking and my focus. The problem for me was I had dug such a deep hole for myself with my personal credit card situation that it took a lot of work with the assistance of energy tools and the knowledge of the universal laws to turn my credit card ocean liner in a different direction.

CHAPTER 24

You Can Experience the Life Style You Want

I have put together a program in Applied Freedom Technologies to assist those who have the desire to live the life they intended when they made the choice to be a physical being in this physical time/space reality. Whether you understand or accept that it was your choice to be where you are now is your decision. What I am offering you is freedom to be, do, and have the things you have already created in your mind and more.

"Bonus Audio Download"

This bonus audio download has been created to assist you in your quest to create the lifestyle you want. It is not a how to guide, because life situations are different and the tools being given can be used in various ways. Most of the sources for the tools have been included (so more detailed instruction is available to you). I would recommend you sign up with one of our AFT mentorship/coaching programs for instruction tailored to your situation. Register on the Applied Freedom Technologies web site to receive your **free** bonus audio download, just log on to "myaft.net" look for Bonus Audio Download to complete the registration.

Basic Principles of Applied Freedom Technologies

1. You must accept the idea that our universe, i.e. this world, is abundant, there are no shortages and there is no lack.

2. You are responsible for your life; all power and control of you is within you.

3. Everything is energy.

4. Everything is in vibration.

Applied Freedom Technologies is a tri-part combination of knowledge, tools, and methods to put you back in touch with who you really are. You are a powerful, wonderfully constructed, whole and perfect being, created by God, source or whoever you choose to believe is the reason you exist. (www.myaft.net)

I know an old Pastor who likes to quote a scripture from Ecclesiastes that states, "…there is nothing new under the sun." The information offered in Applied Freedom Technologies is not new, however it has to my knowledge never been packaged this way. In my own process of learning and testing the techniques in Applied Freedom Technologies, I have developed some innovative approaches which provide better understanding and faster assimilation of the information and tools that are supplied.

The tri-part combinations of information in Applied Freedom Technologies consist of tools and techniques to assist you in controlling your body, mind, and spirit and operating in commerce.

The idea that we as individuals create our own reality is not new. However there are more tools, techniques, and general knowledge about how this works today than in any prior period. It is my belief that by design, information which can be used for general social and economic good for all people has been suppressed, just as in the movie "The Secret." The information I am offering has been and still is for the most part kept a secret.

I find it interesting that the more I give thought to the idea that each one of us has the ability to create and control our own reality, the more it seems so few of us human beings actually take advantage of this knowledge.

We are powerful beings and I believe there could be many reasons why things are the way they are on this earth. Not the least of which is, we as superior beings take on our human form in this earth/time/space reality because we want to experience struggle, pain, hurt, and a variety of negative situations. We want the growth and expansion which is gained from the experience of "bad" things happening to us or to others.

Much of what I would like to express here goes beyond my own ability to totally express in words, so I will not attempt to do that. What I choose to do now is what I think many of you would like to do now, which is live the life that you create and choose for yourself. The possibilities are limitless. For me it is time for only fun, doing only that which is pleasing to me. The principles, tools and techniques put together for you in Applied Freedom Technologies are those which I used to transform my life and they can work for you.

www.ingramcontent.com/pod-product-compliance
Lightning Source LLC
LaVergne TN
LVHW021526080426
835509LV00018B/2680

9780578135533